Body Talk

Control Freak

HORMONES, THE BRAIN, AND THE NERVOUS SYSTEM

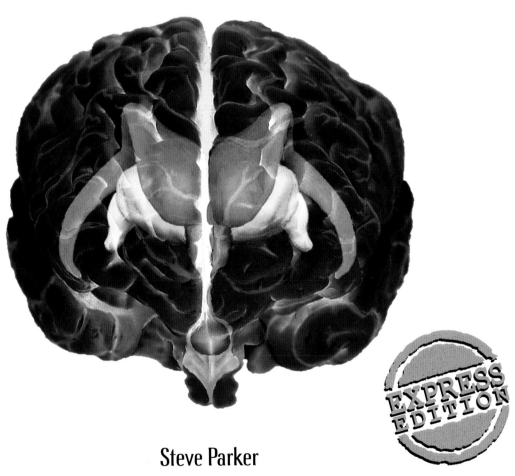

EXPRESS EDITION

Steve Parker

Raintree

Chicago, Illinois

© 2007 Raintree
Published by Raintree, division of
Reed Elsevier, Inc.
Chicago, Illinois

Customer Service   888–363–4266

Visit our website at www.raintreelibrary.com

Printed and bound in China by South China
Printing Company Ltd

10 09 08 07 06
10 9 8 7 6 5 4 3 2 1

**Library of Congress Cataloging-in-
Publication Data**
Parker, Steve.
    Control freak! / Steve Parker.
       p. cm. -- (Body talk)
    Includes index.
    10 digit ISBN 1-4109-2659-1 (lib. bdg.) --
    13 digit ISBN 978-1-4109-2659-3 (lib. bdg.) --
    10 digit ISBN 1-4109-2666-4 (pbk)
    13 digit ISBN 978-1-4109-2666-1 (pbk)
    1. Neurophysiology--Juvenile literature. 2.
Nervous system--Juvenile literature.   I. Title.
II. Series: Parker, Steve. Body talk.
    QP361.5.P3722 2007
    612.8--dc22
                                      2005022269

This leveled text is a version of *Freestyle: Body
Talk: Control Freak*

Acknowledgments
The publishers would like to thank the following
for permission to reproduce photographs:
Action Plus **p. 40** (Glyn Kirk), **p. 6** (Mike Hewitt),
p. 8 (Neil Tingle); Alamy **pp. 36-37, 21**
(Kolvenbach); Corbis **pp. 6-7, 18-19, 34-35; 20**
(Bob Gelberge), **pp. 4-5** (George Hall), **pp. 16-17**
(Tom & Dee Ann McCarthy), **p. 29** (Michael
Kevin Daly), **p. 27** (Varie/Alt), **p. 35** (Creatas);
Getty Images **pp. 20-21; 10** (Joe McNally),
pp. 28-29 (Image Bank), **pp. 5, 24-25, 33,
40-41** (Stone), **p. 43** (Taxi); Harcourt
Education/Tudor Photography **pp. 15, 30-31**;
Science Photo Library **pp. 42; 10-11,
22-23** (AJ Photo), **p. 14** (CNRI), **pp. 26-27**
(Dr M.A. Ansary), **pp. 23, 39** (James Holmes),
p. 39 (Michael Donne), **p. 9** (Pasieka),
pp. 32-33 (TEK Image), **p. 38** (Zephyr),
pp. 12-13 (Superstock).

Cover photograph of head with wires
reproduced with permission of Tips.

The author and publisher would like to thank
Ann Fullick for her assistance in the preparation
of this book.

The paper used to print this book comes from
sustainable resources.

Disclaimer
All the Internet addresses (URLs) given in this
book were valid at the time of going to press.
However, due to the dynamic nature of the
Internet, some addresses may have changed, or
sites may have ceased to exist since publication.
While the author and publishers regret any
inconvenience this may cause readers, no
responsibility for an such changes can be
accepted by either the author or the publishers.

Dedicated to the memory of Lucy Owen

Contents

Any words appearing in the text in bold, **like this**, are explained in the Glossary. You can also look out for them in "Body language" at the bottom of each page.

Total Control

Controlling the body

sense organs (eyes, ears, nose, tongue, skin)
– these pick up, or detect, what is going on outside the body

brain
– the body's control center

nerves
– these carry signals between the brain and the body

hormones
– they control growth or affect the way body parts work

You are blasting through the sky in a supersonic jet plane. This jet can fly faster than sound. You are traveling at incredible speed.

You need to stay totally focused. You need your **senses** to be sharp. Senses are the body's ways of **detecting** sound, light, and other things around you. Your eyes keep checking the dials and controls. Your hands feel the control stick. Your ears hear messages through a headset.

senses   the body's ways of detecting things such as light, temperature, or sound

The brain in the plane

This information from your senses feeds into your brain. Your brain is an amazing machine. Every second you make decisions. You decide on speed, height, and direction. If you get it wrong, you might crash the plane.

Find out later ...

... what your brain does while you are asleep.

... why children and adults like different flavors.

... what happens when you are scared.

▼ A pilot's senses are extra sharp. His brain must be in complete command.

hormones chemicals that spread around the body in the blood and affect different body parts

Control Center

Your brain is a dome-shaped lump of jelly. It has deep grooves and wrinkles in its surface. There is a stalk at its base.

The brain may not look impressive. But it is an amazing place. It is where you think. It is where you store memories. Your brain controls your movements. It is where you have feelings like sadness and joy. In many ways your brain is YOU.

Protect it

The brain is soft and delicate. It is protected by the hard **skull** bone around it. Sometimes the brain needs extra protection. Then you should wear a helmet or hard hat. You should wear one for activities such as climbing, cycling, or tobogganing (right).

This scanner image shows ➤ a living brain. There are thin, cushionlike layers around it. These are called **meninges**. They help protect the brain.

Body language meninges   three thin layers around the brain and spinal cord that protect and nourish them

Size doesn't matter

Different people may have different sized brains. But the size of a brain has nothing to do with intelligence. It's what you do with it that matters.

Exercising your body can make your muscles more powerful. You can also exercise your brain. Learning and remembering are good exercises. So is problem solving. They help to increase your brain power.

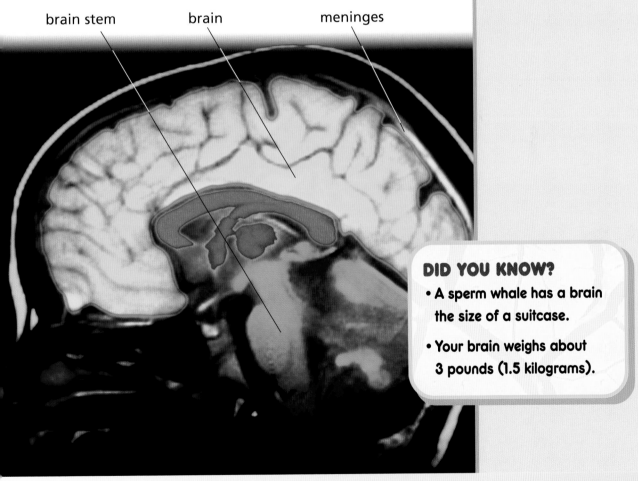

brain stem   brain   meninges

Where did you get that idea?

Your brain has several main parts. The biggest part is called the **cerebrum**. This is the wrinkled dome at the top. It is where you have most of your thoughts and ideas.

▼ The brain has many parts. Each does different jobs. All the parts work together.

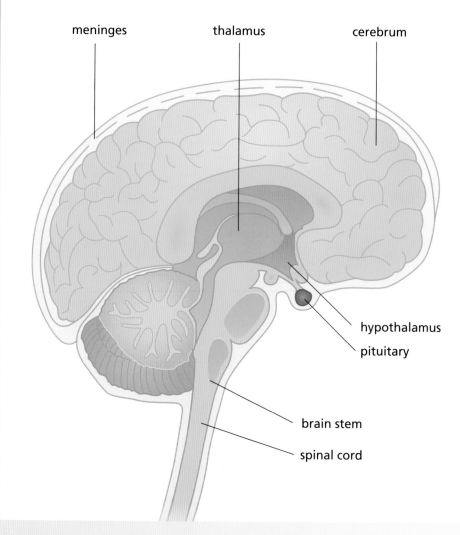

meninges

thalamus

cerebrum

hypothalamus

pituitary

brain stem

spinal cord

cerebrum   large upper part of the brain. Inside it are nerve fibers. It is the main part of the brain.

Inner parts

The middle part of the brain is shaped like two eggs. This is the **thalamus**. It helps control sleep. It helps control if you are tired or fully awake. It also receives information from the **senses**.

Small but important

Just below the thalamus is an area called the **hypothalamus**. It is only the size of a grape. But this is where feelings like hunger, anger, and joy are based.

Brain bricks

All body parts are made of **cells**. Cells are tiny "building blocks." The brain contains billions of cells called **nerve cells**. Each nerve cell has long "arms" (below). They pass on messages.

TOO MANY TO IMAGINE

- There are more than 100 billion nerve cells in the brain

- Up to 10,000 brain cells die every day. There are so many cells left, it hardly matters.

nerve cell cell that receives and sends on messages

Think!

The **cerebral cortex** is a thin covering. It covers the **cerebrum**. The cerebrum is the main part of the brain. You use the cortex every time you think, look, and listen. You use it when you move.

If you could spread out the cortex, it would be as large as a pillowcase. But it has lots of deep folds and wrinkles. They make it fit inside your skull.

No-pain brain!

The brain cannot feel pain or touch. This means that people can be wide awake during a brain operation (below).

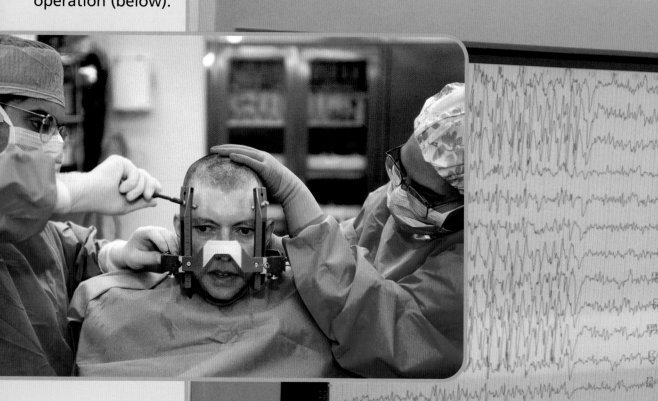

cerebrum large upper part of the brain. Inside it are nerve fibers. It is the main part of the brain.

Gray and white

The cortex is what we call our "mind." It is the main place for our thoughts and awareness. The cortex is colored gray. It is sometimes called "gray matter."

Underneath the cortex is "white matter." This contains long, wire-like fibers. The fibers link the cortex to other parts of your brain.

Left or right?

The main brain has two halves. The left side deals with words, numbers, science skills, and problems. The right side deals with shapes, colors, sounds, and imagination. Which side do you use most?

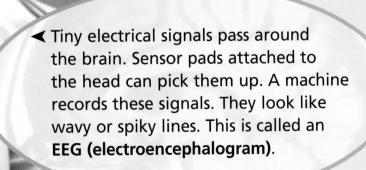

◄ Tiny electrical signals pass around the brain. Sensor pads attached to the head can pick them up. A machine records these signals. They look like wavy or spiky lines. This is called an **EEG (electroencephalogram)**.

Memories are made of ... what?

Try to remember a happy time. Is this memory just scenes? Or can you also remember sounds, smells, and feelings? The more you think back, the more you can remember.

The nerve message pathways

Your brain has millions of **nerve cells**. These are tiny parts that make up the brain. They are linked together in trillions of ways. A memory is probably a set of links between nerve cells. These links carry a nerve message along a certain path.

Short-term memories

The brain keeps some memories for just a few minutes or hours. These are usually unimportant memories, such as what we ate for lunch. We forget them. Otherwise the brain would be full of unimportant information.

Our strongest memories ➤ are usually exciting or strange events. These might be times that have seemed very good, very bad, or very scary!

nerve cell   cell that receives and sends on messages

If you use a memory often, you keep the path open. The links stay strong. The memory stays strong. Memories that are not used much fade away. The links are lost.

Memory centers

Memories are stored in the outer layer of the brain. This is called the **cerebral cortex**. They are also stored in parts inside the brain.

Long-term memories

The brain stores some memories for almost a lifetime. They include very important information. They include our names, happy events, and sad events.

cerebral cortex gray layer covering the cerebrum. It is involved in thinking, memory, the senses, movement, and other activities.

The Body's Network

What a nerve!

The **spinal cord** is your main nerve. It carries information between your brain and your body. The spinal cord starts at the base of your brain. It runs down inside the bones of your neck and back.

The brain receives and sends messages all the time. This is how it controls body parts. This is also how it makes the parts work together.

The messages are sent as tiny pulses of electricity (a form of **energy**). These messages pass along wire-like parts called **nerves**. Nerves link the brain to all parts of the body.

brain

spinal cord

The body's nerves go from ▲ the brain and the spinal cord. They go to every part of the body.

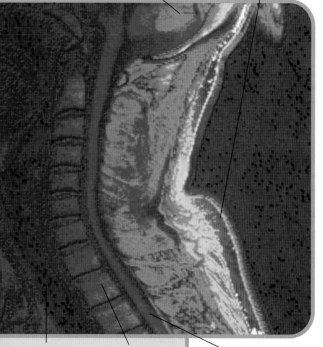

base of brain

skin on back of neck

windpipe   back bones   spinal cord

Body language   energy   ability to cause changes and make things happen

Messengers

Nerves look like pieces of bendy, gray string. Inside each nerve is a bundle of fibers. These are called nerve fibers. They carry the nerve messages.

GET ON YOUR NERVES

- If all the nerves in your body could be joined end to end, they would stretch around the world twice
- Your spinal cord is about as thick as your little finger.

Pins and needles

If you sit awkwardly for a while, you may feel a horrible tingling. This is known as "pins and needles." It may happen because a nerve is squashed. The nerve gets back to normal when you rub and stretch. Then the feeling goes away.

Info in and info out

Some **nerves** only carry messages into the brain. These are called **sensory nerves**. The nerves that run from your eyes are sensory nerves.

Other nerves only carry messages from your brain to your muscles. These are called **motor** nerves. The nerve to your voice box is one. It makes you speak.

Mixed nerves carry messages both ways. The nerve to your tongue is a mixed nerve. It sends messages to the brain about taste. The same nerve tells your tongue to move.

Nerve messages

Some nerve messages travel quite slowly. They travel at just 7 feet (2 meters) per second. Others go much faster. They may travel over 330 feet (100 meters) per second.

Sense organs are body parts ➤ that **detect** lights, sounds, smells, tastes, and touches. They pass messages to the brain. Then we know what is happening around us.

sensory nerve   nerve that carries messages from a sense organ to the brain

Control centers

Something touches your skin. Nerves send messages to the brain. Then you realize something is touching you. But where in your brain do these messages go?

They go to the touch center. This is a part of the brain's outer layer, or **cerebral cortex**.

There are many other centers in the cortex (see diagram below). Each does a special job. These jobs include seeing, hearing, and moving. They also include understanding words and speaking.

Brain damage

Sometimes a head injury damages parts of the brain. For example, a person might suffer damage to the hearing center in the brain. Then he or she is not able to hear.

- touch
- taste
- understanding vision
- vision (sight)
- understanding and choosing words
- movement
- planning movements
- speech area
- awareness
- hearing

motor   to do with movements, muscles, and the nerves controlling them

Running on Auto

Some of the most important things that your body does seem to happen "by themselves." You don't have to think about breathing. You don't think about making your heart beat. But your brain controls them, too.

Automatic control

The brain stem has its own control centers (see below). They control heartbeat and breathing. They also control many other processes inside the body.

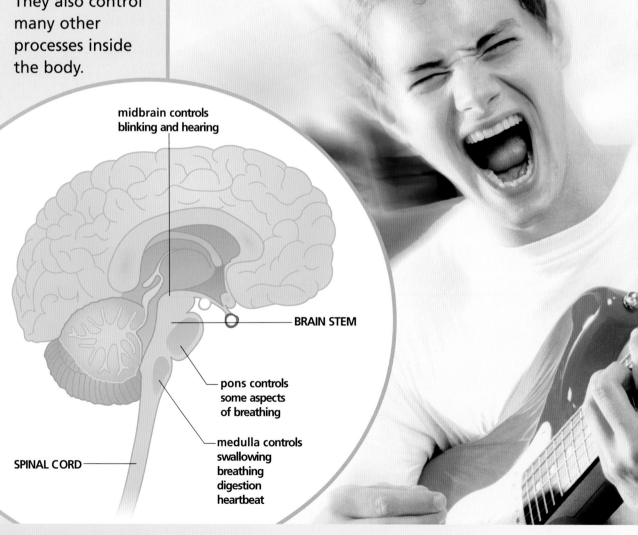

midbrain controls blinking and hearing

BRAIN STEM

pons controls some aspects of breathing

medulla controls swallowing breathing digestion heartbeat

SPINAL CORD

automatically   acting or happening without having to think about it

Two brains in one?

It may seem as if we have two brains. There is the thinking mind. Then there is the brain that controls things **automatically**. This means that we don't have to think about doing them.

The thinking mind is mainly in the upper parts of the brain. Automatic control happens in the lower parts. It happens mainly in the **brain stem**. This is the stalk at the base of your brain.

◄ Playing an instrument and singing at the same time is hard. Imagine if you also had to remember to make your heart beat and to breathe! Luckily your brain controls these things automatically.

brain stem   lowest part of the brain, where automatic actions are controlled. Its lower end forms part of the spinal cord.

Look out!

You are reading quietly. A big spider crawls across your page. You might jump up and shout. This shows how fast the brain can make reactions. It can make your body leap in less than a second.

Auto-reactions

Some types of body reactions finish before you realize they have started. These are called **reflexes**.

We probably blink our eyes more than 30,000 times every day. Each blink is a reflex. It washes away dirt and germs. Sneezing is another reflex. We sneeze to clear dust from our noses.

Saved from danger

You accidentally touch a sharp point or hot object. You quickly move away from the danger. You move without thinking. This is a reflex.

Bundles of reflexes

New babies haven't learned to control their bodies. Their actions are mainly reflexes. They cry if they are hungry. They throw out their arms if you startle them.

reflex   automatic reaction, such as coughing or blinking

Reflexes help to keep you safe. They don't involve the brain. They happen immediately. Reflexes are controlled by nerves in a particular part of the body.

▼ A ball comes toward your head. You **automatically** close your eyes. You twist away. These are reflex reactions. Your body is trying to protect your eyes and face. It is very hard not to do this!

Fast reactions

When sprinters begin a race, their ears hear the starting sound. The message passes to their brains. Then their brains send messages to their leg muscles. Sprinters with the fastest reactions have a better chance of winning.

automatically   acting or happening without having to think about it

21

Awake and Asleep

You spend about one-third of your life asleep. Does your brain switch off when you sleep? No. It is just as busy as when you are awake. Millions of **nerve** messages pass around the sleeping brain. But they are different kinds of signals.

"Sleep testing" is often ➤ used to understand sleep patterns and dreaming.

Re-running the day

Your body rests as you sleep. It also repairs itself. So what is your busy brain doing? Perhaps it goes through the memories of the day. It may sort the memories into important or not. Then it can forget the less important ones. This leaves memory space for the rest.

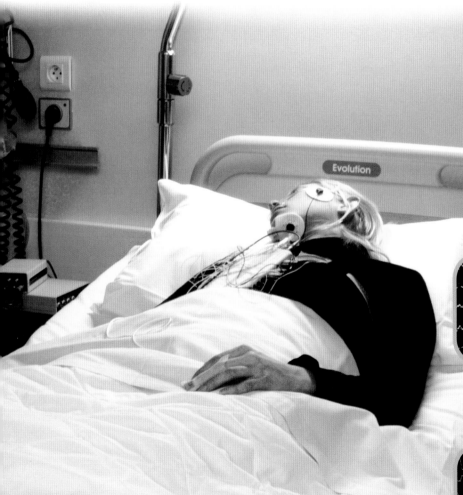

Changing brainwaves

The **EEG** machine (see page 11) picks up nerve signals in the brain. It records them as up-and-down patterns. These "brain waves" are different when we are wide awake from when we are dozy or asleep.

At different times "brain waves" can be small...

... or tall and wide.

EEG (electro-encephalogram) record of electrical activity in the brain made using special equipment

A new baby usually needs 18–20 hours of sleep. A ten-year-old usually needs 10–11 hours. Most adults need about 7–8 hours.

Zzzzzz ...

You fall asleep. Soon you go into a deep sleep. Your muscles are relaxed. Your heartbeat and breathing slow down.

Flickering eyes

After about an hour, your muscles tense and twitch. Your eyes flick backward and forward. This is called **REM (Rapid Eye Movement) sleep.**

After another 30–60 minutes you go back to deep sleep. This is called **non-REM, or NREM, sleep.** While you sleep you change several times. You keep going from REM sleep to deep sleep.

Dreams

People who are woken from REM sleep nearly always remember dreaming. People woken during deep sleep (NREM sleep) rarely remember any dreams.

We do not really know why we have different types of sleep. We don't really know why we dream.

REM (Rapid Eye Movement) sleep   period of sleep when the body is less relaxed. The eyes flicker and dreams occur.

Lack of sleep

If we don't get enough sleep, we feel tired. Lack of sleep can cause headaches. It can also cause memory loss.

▲ Some people fall asleep almost anywhere. This happens when we are very young and very active. It can also happen when we've had a late night.

NREM (non-REM) sleep period of deep sleep when the body is very relaxed. The heartbeat is slow and there are no dreams.

Sense-ational!

Your body has five main **senses**. You have a nose for smell. You have a tongue for taste. Your skin is for touch. You have eyes for sight and ears for hearing.

Each sense picks up changes in your surroundings. It sends **nerve** messages to your brain. Your brain takes in this information. Then it decides what to do.

What a sight!

For most people sight is the main sense. We use it to get around and do daily tasks. We use it for taking in information.

Inside the eye

The eye's **lens** (see below) brings things clearly into view. It shines an image onto the **retina**. This is at the back of the eye. It sends nerve messages to the brain.

Light passes into the ➤ eye through the pupil. It passes into the eyeball.

lens

iris

pupil

eye moving muscle

optic nerve

retina

muscle

lens   pea-sized part of the eye behind the pupil. It bends or focuses light onto the inside of the eyeball.

Bright eyes

Light shines into your eye. It comes in through the dark hole. This is called the **pupil**. When the light is dim, your pupils open wide. They let in as much light as possible.

In bright light the pupils shrink. They reduce the light coming in. This protects sensitive cells at the back of your eye.

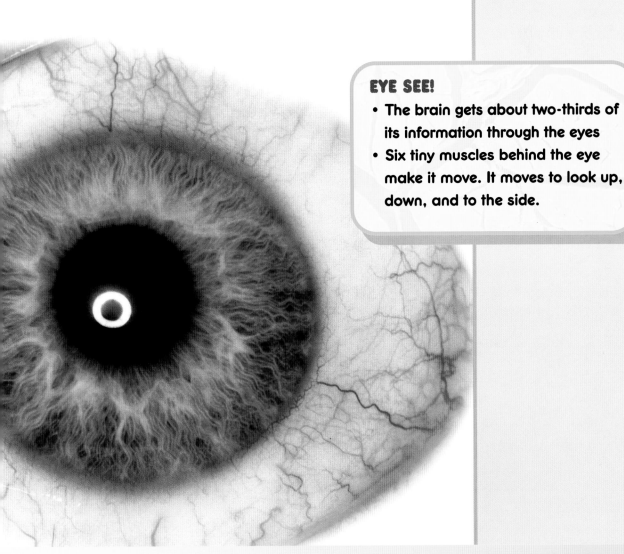

EYE SEE!
- The brain gets about two-thirds of its information through the eyes
- Six tiny muscles behind the eye make it move. It moves to look up, down, and to the side.

retina   thin lining at the back of the eyeball

How you hear

Sound waves travel into the ear canal (see below). They make the eardrum vibrate. Vibrations then pass along three ear bones. They reach the **cochlea**. Here they change into nerve messages. These go to your brain.

All ears

Sit still and quiet. Listen hard. What can you hear? There are usually sounds of some kind. There may be sounds of people or traffic. There may be sounds of wind or birds.
Your ears pick up these noises. They send **nerve** messages to your brain.

We shut our eyes if light is ➤ too bright. We have to cover our ears with our hands if a noise is too loud.

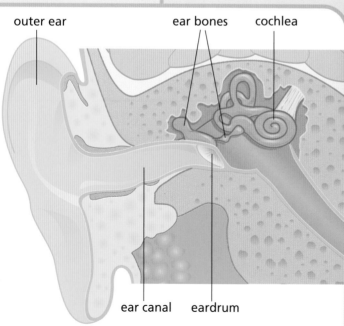

outer ear   ear bones   cochlea

ear canal   eardrum

cochlea   small, snail-shaped part in the ear. It changes movement or vibrations into nerve messages.

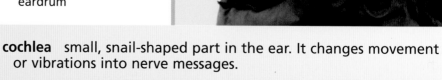

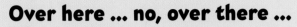

Over here ... no, over there ...

Sounds travel as invisible "waves." A sound coming from the right reaches your right ear first. It hits the left ear about 1/1000th of a second later.

Sounds also lose loudness as they travel. So sound from the right is louder in your right ear than in your left.

Your brain picks up these tiny differences in time and loudness. They help the brain work out where sound is coming from. This is called **stereophonic** hearing.

WARNING!

Too much loud noise can damage the delicate ear. This is why there are laws about sound levels. Sound levels are measured in decibels (dB).

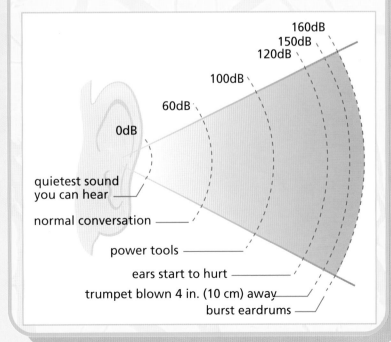

160dB
150dB
120dB
100dB
60dB
0dB

quietest sound you can hear
normal conversation
power tools
ears start to hurt
trumpet blown 4 in. (10 cm) away
burst eardrums

stereophonic able to detect the direction of a sound because of the slight differences heard by the right and left ears

29

Sniff ... what's that smell?

What was the last strong smell you remember? Flowers? Last night's dinner?

Smells can bring back strong memories and feelings. This is because **nerve** messages from your nose go to particular parts of your brain. These parts are also involved in feelings and memories.

Why smells seem to fade

You detect a strong smell. After a while it seems to fade. But maybe the smell is still there.

The smell's nerve messages stop going into your thoughts. The brain stops them. This is because a smell is not important after you have **detected** it. It is more important to be aware of new smells.

Keeping your mind clear

The same thing happens with your other **senses.** Think about the new sounds of a school. After a while you don't notice them. This way your mind isn't full of unimportant information. You are only aware of new or changed sensations.

How you smell

Your nostrils lead to two spaces. These are called the **nasal chambers** (below). Smelly particles enter these spaces. From here nerve messages pass to the brain.

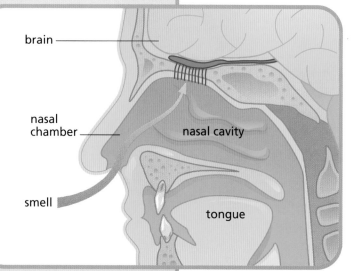

brain

nasal chamber

nasal cavity

smell

tongue

senses the body's ways of detecting things such as light, temperature, or sound

We hate the smells that come from rotten food and animal droppings. Our senses are warning us to stay away from these smells. If we don't, we could catch a disease.

nasal chambers hollow parts between the nostrils and the upper throat. This is where smells are detected.

Terrific tastes

If we take time to eat, we can enjoy the taste of food. We can also enjoy the feel of the food. We can tell whether it is crunchy, lumpy, or creamy. We can tell how hot or cold it is. This is because we have the **sense** of touch inside our mouths.

As you chew, food smells pass to the back of your mouth. They enter your **nasal chambers**. This is where you have the sense of smell.

On the tip of my tongue

Some scientists believe that different parts of your tongue pick up different flavors (see below). The tip of your tongue senses sweet tastes best. The back picks up bitter tastes like coffee.

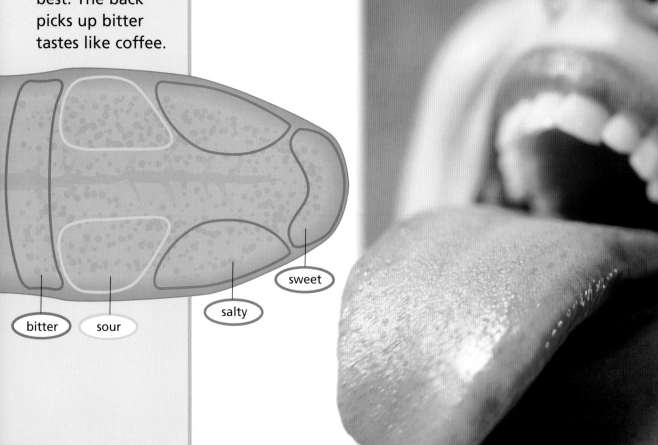

bitter

sour

salty

sweet

nasal chambers   hollow parts between the nostrils and the upper throat. This is where smells are detected.

What you think of as taste is really a mix of senses. It is taste, smell, and touch all working together.

Tongue's tasks

Your tongue doesn't just taste your food. It moves food around your mouth. Your tongue also moves when you talk. It helps you to speak clearly. Try saying "hello" without moving your tongue!

◄ You taste with your tongue's 10,000 **taste buds**. Particles of food stick to the taste buds. The taste buds send messages to the brain.

Changing tastes

Taste buds gradually die away over the years. This is why tastes and flavors seem stronger to young people than to older people.

taste buds   ball-shaped groups of cells on the tongue that detect tastes

Getting in touch

The sense of touch is based in your skin. Touch can give you lots of different information.

Imagine your eyes are closed. You have to guess what an object is. You can only use touch. You feel for the size and shape of the object. Is it smooth or lumpy? You press to see if the object is hard or soft. Is it warm or cold? Your skin senses all these things.

Inside skin

Micro-sensors (below) detect touch. These are nerve endings just under the skin. Some sensors feel light touch. Others sense pressure and pain.

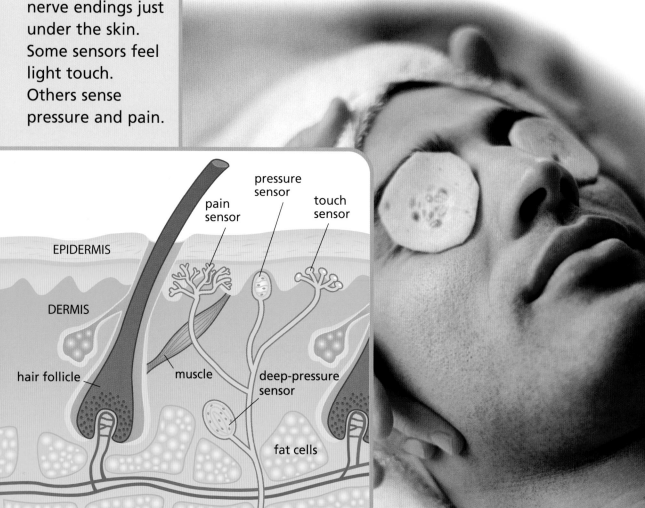

EPIDERMIS

DERMIS

pain sensor

pressure sensor

touch sensor

hair follicle

muscle

deep-pressure sensor

fat cells

micro-sensors   microscopic nerve endings in skin that detect touch

Fingertips and lips

You would probably use your fingers to do this test. Fingers are very sensitive for touch. So are eyelids, lips, and tongues.

All these parts have lots of **micro-sensors**. These are **nerve** endings. They **detect** touch. Other areas of skin are not so sensitive.

Ouch!

Our skin can also detect pain. We don't like pain. But we need it. Pain warns us that our body is getting damaged. Then we can protect ourselves.

Itchy-scratchy

Why does skin feel an itch? It might be a tiny insect walking (below). It could be one of the skin's hairs rubbing the surface. A quick scratch usually works.

◀ Touch affects our mood. A gentle massage or stroking can calm us. Other touches may be funny or scary.

detect pick up

35

Chemical Control

Your brain is your body's boss. It controls most body parts. It controls them by sending messages along **nerves**. But there is another control system, too. This system uses **hormones**. These are chemicals made in parts of your body.

There are dozens of different hormones. Each affects different body processes. Hormones control how the body grows. They also control how the body repairs damage.

Hormone glands

Some hormone glands make just one hormone. Others produce several.

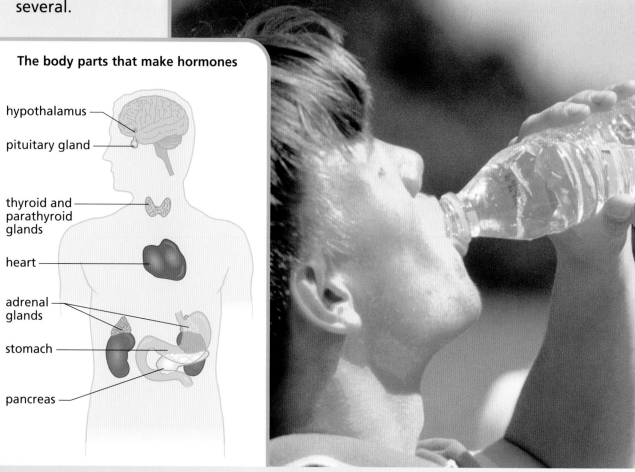

The body parts that make hormones

- hypothalamus
- pituitary gland
- thyroid and parathyroid glands
- heart
- adrenal glands
- stomach
- pancreas

hormones   chemicals that spread around the body in the blood and affect different body parts

Where are hormones made?

Hormones are made in parts of the body called **endocrine glands** (see diagram, page 36). The blood stream carries the hormones to different body parts. Then they control how those parts work. More hormones usually make the part work faster.

Stress

Sometimes we feel nervous or worried. It happens partly because there are more hormones in the blood. These are called stress hormones.

HORMONES ON TARGET

- Some hormones control just a few body parts. This might be the heart or the stomach
- Other hormones affect almost every cell in your body.

◄ Hormones control water in the body. If there is not enough water, they reduce the amount of urine. Then you begin to feel thirsty.

endocrine glands parts that make hormones

Hormone control center

The **pituitary** gland is the boss of your **hormone** system. It produces more than ten hormones. Most of these control other hormone glands.

Double control

The pituitary doesn't work alone. It is joined to the **hypothalamus**. This is part of the brain.

The hypothalamus tells the pituitary when to release hormones. It does this by sending **nerve** messages and chemicals.

Twin tasks

The **pancreas** makes juices that **digest** food. It also makes two hormones. These control the amount of glucose sugar in your blood. **Blood glucose** is sugar we get from broken down food.

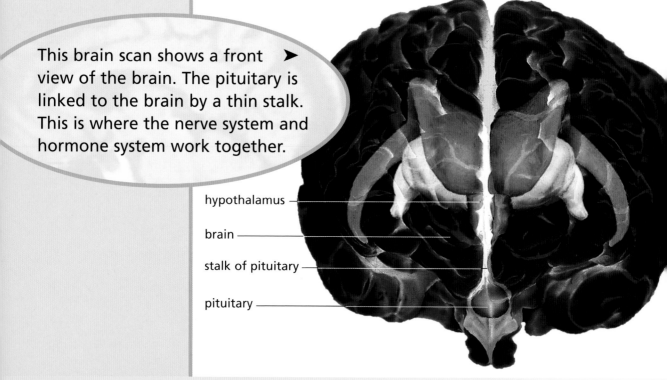

This brain scan shows a front ➤ view of the brain. The pituitary is linked to the brain by a thin stalk. This is where the nerve system and hormone system work together.

hypothalamus ———

brain ———

stalk of pituitary ———

pituitary ———

Body language   pancreas   part that makes juices for digestion and hormones. These hormones control the level of blood glucose.

In the neck

The **thyroid** is in your neck. It makes hormones that control how fast your body **cells** work. Sometimes the thyroid goes wrong. This can make the body work too slow. Or it can make the body work too fast. These problems can usually be treated with medicines.

Diabetes

Some people suffer from diabetes. This is when the body doesn't make enough **insulin**. Insulin is a hormone. It controls blood glucose (see page 38). Diabetic people may need to inject insulin. Otherwise they might collapse.

◄ People with diabetes have to be careful about what they eat. They may also need regular injections.

insulin hormone made by the pancreas. It lowers the level of blood glucose.

Run for it!

Can you remember what it's like to feel afraid? Your heart thumps. Your skin goes sweaty. Your muscles tense. Your body gets ready to move fast. These changes are partly caused by **nerve** messages. They are also caused by a **hormone** called **adrenaline**.

Through the "pain barrier"

Some athletes carry on even when they are exhausted or injured. They don't seem to notice the pain. This is because of adrenaline and other hormones.

Some people like the ➤ excitement of being scared. These feelings are brought on by nerves and the hormone adrenaline.

hormones   chemicals that spread around the body in the blood and affect different body parts

A big buzz

Adrenaline is made in two hormone glands. These are called **adrenals**.

Adrenaline gets your body ready for action. It changes how your blood flows. More blood rushes to the muscles. Less blood goes to your skin and stomach. This is why you look pale when you are scared. It is why you get a tight feeling in your stomach.

This is how adrenaline and nerves get your body ready to fight or run away:

- Heart beats faster
- Lungs breathe faster
- More blood flows to muscles
- Skin sweats
- Senses become extra sharp.

Oh, grow up!

Slow processes in the body are usually controlled by **hormones**. Growing from a baby to an adult takes about 20 years. The main hormone affecting growth is called growth hormone. It is made in the **pituitary** gland (see the diagram on page 36).

Up and up

Some people grow faster than others. These people have slightly more growth hormone than others.

Changing bones

Growing does not just mean getting bigger. As you grow, your bones change shape. They become harder. This is mainly controlled by hormones.

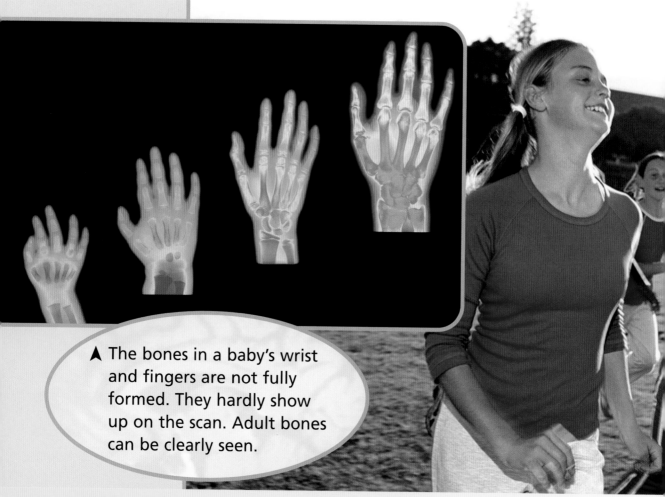

▲ The bones in a baby's wrist and fingers are not fully formed. They hardly show up on the scan. Adult bones can be clearly seen.

pituitary the main endocrine gland. It is located at the base of the brain.

People with slightly less growth hormone take longer to reach their adult height. This is one of the normal differences between people.

Too much, too little

In a few people, the pituitary makes too much growth hormone. Then the body grows extra fast. In some others the pituitary makes too little. Their bodies stay small. Luckily these problems can be treated with medicines.

▼ These young people are all about the same age. But they are different heights. This is partly because of the effects of growth hormone.

Find Out More

Books

Parker, Steve. *The Brain and Nervous System.* Chicago: Raintree, 2004

Newquist, H.P. *The Great Brain Book: An Inside Look at the Inside of Your Head.* New York: Scholastic, 2005

The Brain: Our Nervous System, Seymour Simon New York: HarperCollins 2006

World Wide Web

The Internet can tell you more about your body and your brain. You can use a search engine or search directory.

Type in keywords such as:

- eardrum
- retina
- nervous system
- brain
- sleep and dreaming
- hormones

Search tips

There are billions of pages on the Internet. It can be difficult to find what you are looking for.

These search skills will help you find useful websites more quickly:

- Know exactly what you want to find out about.
- Use two to six keywords in a search. Put the most important words first.
- Only use names of people, places, or things.

Where to search

Search engine

A search engine looks through millions of pages. It lists all the sites that match the words in the search box. You will find the best matches are at the top of the list, on the first page. Try **www.google.com**

Search directory

A person instead of a computer has sorted a search directory. You can search by keyword or subject and browse through the different sites. It is like looking through books on a library shelf. Try **yahooligans.com**

Glossary

adrenaline hormone that gets the body ready for action

adrenals two glands on top of the kidneys. They make several hormones including adrenaline.

automatically acting or happening without having to think about it

blood glucose sugar obtained when food is broken down. Blood glucose is the body's main source of energy.

brain stem lowest part of the brain, where automatic actions are controlled. Its lower end forms part of the spinal cord.

cells microscopic "building blocks" that make up all body parts

cerebral cortex gray layer covering the cerebrum. It is involved in thinking, memory, the senses, movement, and other activities.

cerebrum large upper part of the brain. Inside it are nerve fibers. It is the main part of the brain.

cochlea small, snail-shaped part in the ear. It changes movement or vibrations into nerve messages.

detect pick up

digest break down food into smaller and smaller pieces

EEG (electroencephalogram) record of electrical activity in the brain made using special equipment

endocrine glands parts that make hormones

energy ability to cause changes and make things happen

hormones chemicals that spread around the body in the blood and affect different body parts

hypothalamus small part of the brain that deals with emotions and automatic processes

insulin hormone made by the pancreas. It lowers the level of blood glucose.

lens pea-sized part of the eye behind the pupil. It bends or focuses light onto the inside of the eyeball.

meninges three thin layers around the brain and spinal cord that protect and nourish them

micro-sensors microscopic nerve endings in skin that detect touch

motor to do with movements, muscles, and the nerves controlling them

nasal chambers hollow parts between the nostrils and the upper throat. This is where smells are detected.

nerve cell cell that receives and sends on messages

nerves wirelike parts that carry messages around the body as tiny pulses of electricity

NREM (Non-Rapid Eye Movement) sleep period of deep sleep when the body is very relaxed. The heartbeat is slow and there are no dreams.

pancreas part that makes juices for digestion and hormones. These hormones control the level of blood glucose.

parathyroid glands glands in the neck that make hormones

pituitary the main endocrine gland. It is located at the base of the brain.

pupil hole that lets light into the eye

reflex automatic reaction such as coughing or blinking

REM (Rapid Eye Movement) sleep period of sleep when the body is less relaxed. The eyes flicker and dreams occur.

retina thin lining at the back of the eyeball

sense organs body parts, such as the nose, used in the senses

senses the body's ways of detecting things such as light, temperature, or sound

sensory nerve nerve that carries messages from a sense organ to the brain

skull main bone in the head, which is really more than 20 bones joined together

spinal cord main nerve linking the brain to the rest of the body

stereophonic able to detect the direction of a sound because of the slight differences heard by the right and left ears

taste buds ball-shaped groups of cells on the tongue that detect tastes

thalamus part in the brain, involved in awareness, sensing the surroundings, memory, and other mental activities

thyroid endocrine gland in the neck

ventricles spaces inside a body part

Index